Usborne
Space
Maze Book

Illustrated by
Emi Ordás, Andrew Kolb,
Fermín Solís and Lauren Ellis

Designed by
Claire Thomas and Ruth Russell

Written by Sam Smith

The mazes at the beginning of the
book are easier and they get more
challenging as you go through.
You'll find solutions to all the
mazes on pages 61-64.

Alien evasion

The astronauts need to clamber back across the ridges and canyons to their spacecraft, but they mustn't disturb the aliens. Which way should they go?

Into the blast zone

Help Mick drive to every workshop to collect his tools before entering the blast zone to service the rocket. He can't take any road twice.

Workshops look like this.

Blast Zone

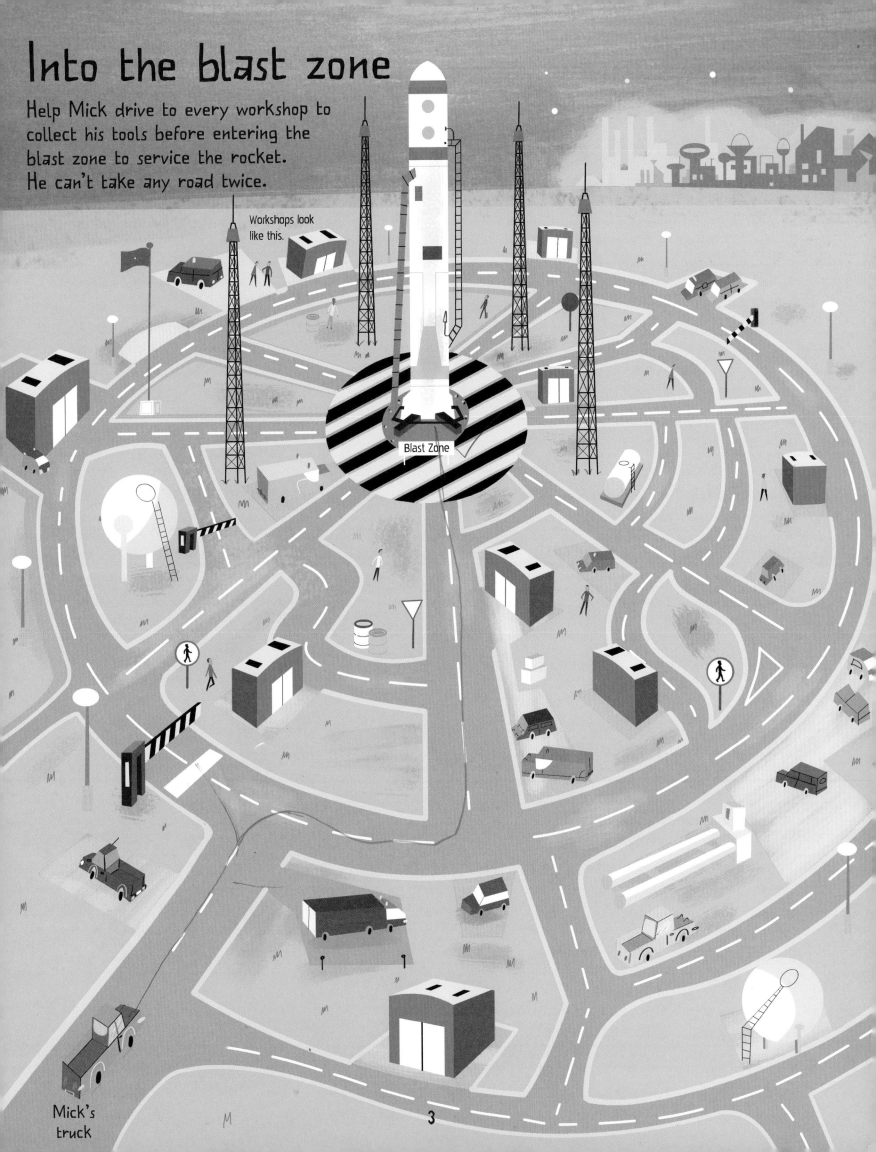

Mick's truck

Metropolis skyline

Steer the Skyline Express along the correct route between the city's high-rise buildings to pick up the people waiting at Metropolis Station.

Skyline Express

Metropolis Station

Spacewalk tangle

One of the astronauts fixing the telescope has forgotten her screwdriver. Which line must Finn follow to take it to her?

Finn

Cosmic racers

Only one of the three competitors can reach the finish and win the Space Race gold cup. Find out who it will be, and trace the route they must take.

Fly the flag

Guide astronaut Alice along the trails of footprints to join Jack, so she can plant the flag on the Moon at the spot marked X.

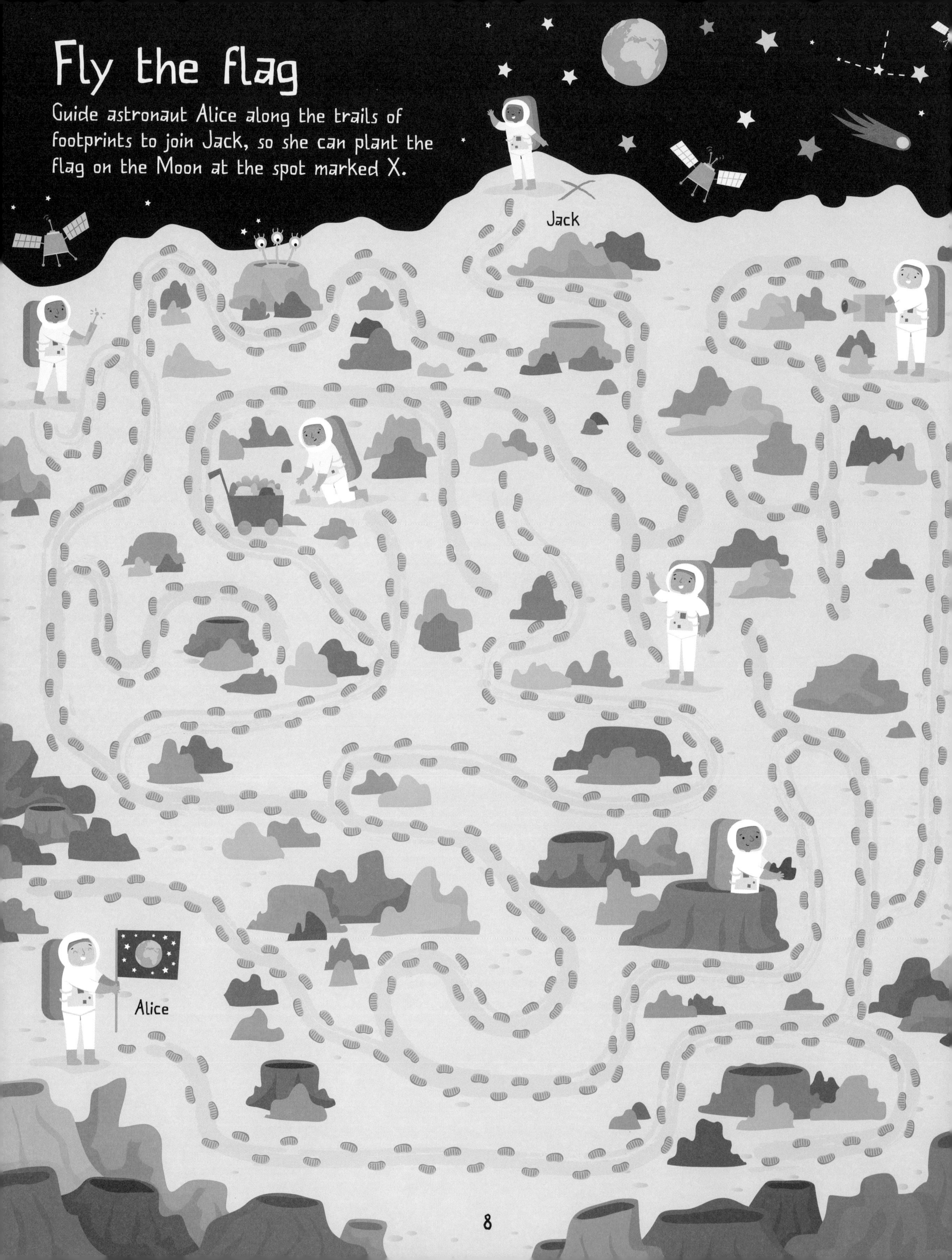

Jack

Alice

Dish dilemma

Help the engineer service each radio telescope on his way to the base, without going down any of the white roads twice.

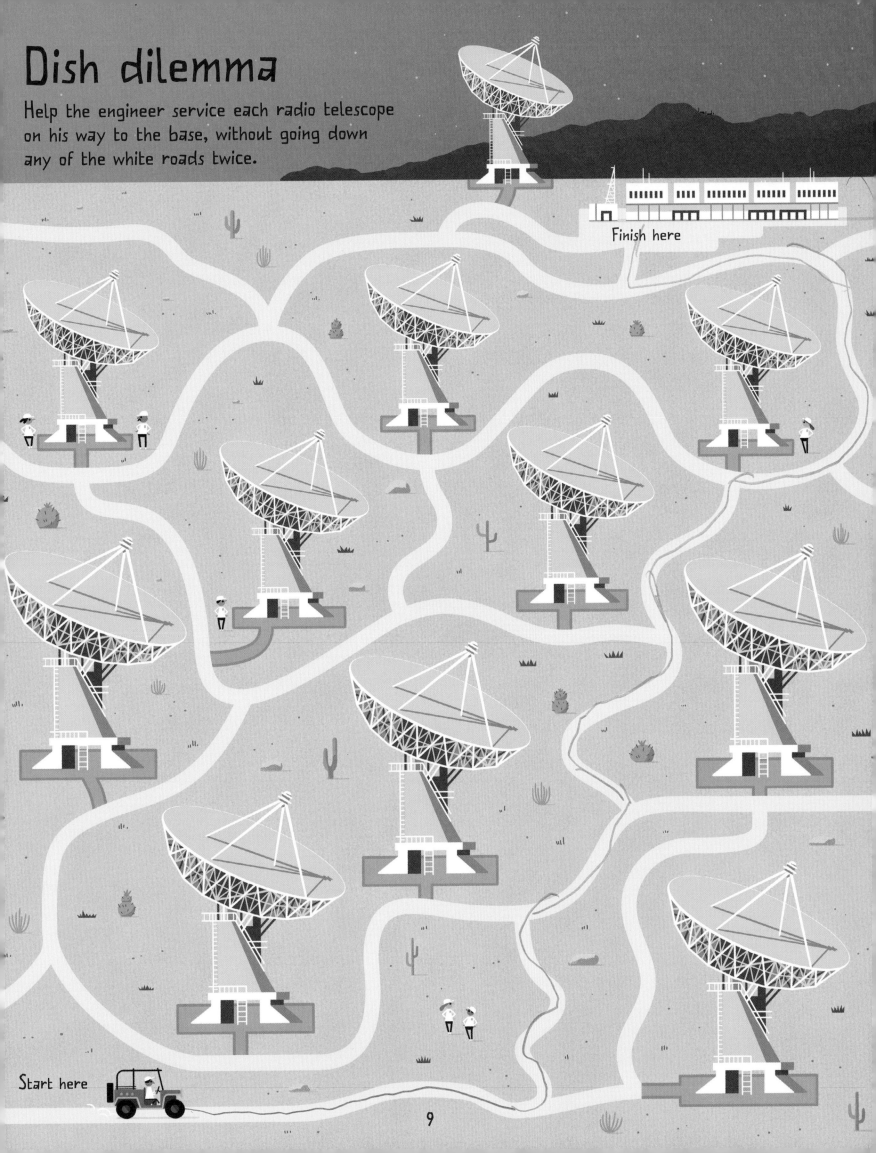

Finish here

Start here

Chasm quandary

Alex is due at work in the lab, but the paths between the icy cliffs are crawling with menacing aliens. Can you find a safe path?

Alex

Lab

Spaceport dash

Mr. and Mrs. Alien have a flight to catch, but they've lost their way. Can you find the right route along the roads so they make it to the spaceport on time?

Start here

Spaceport

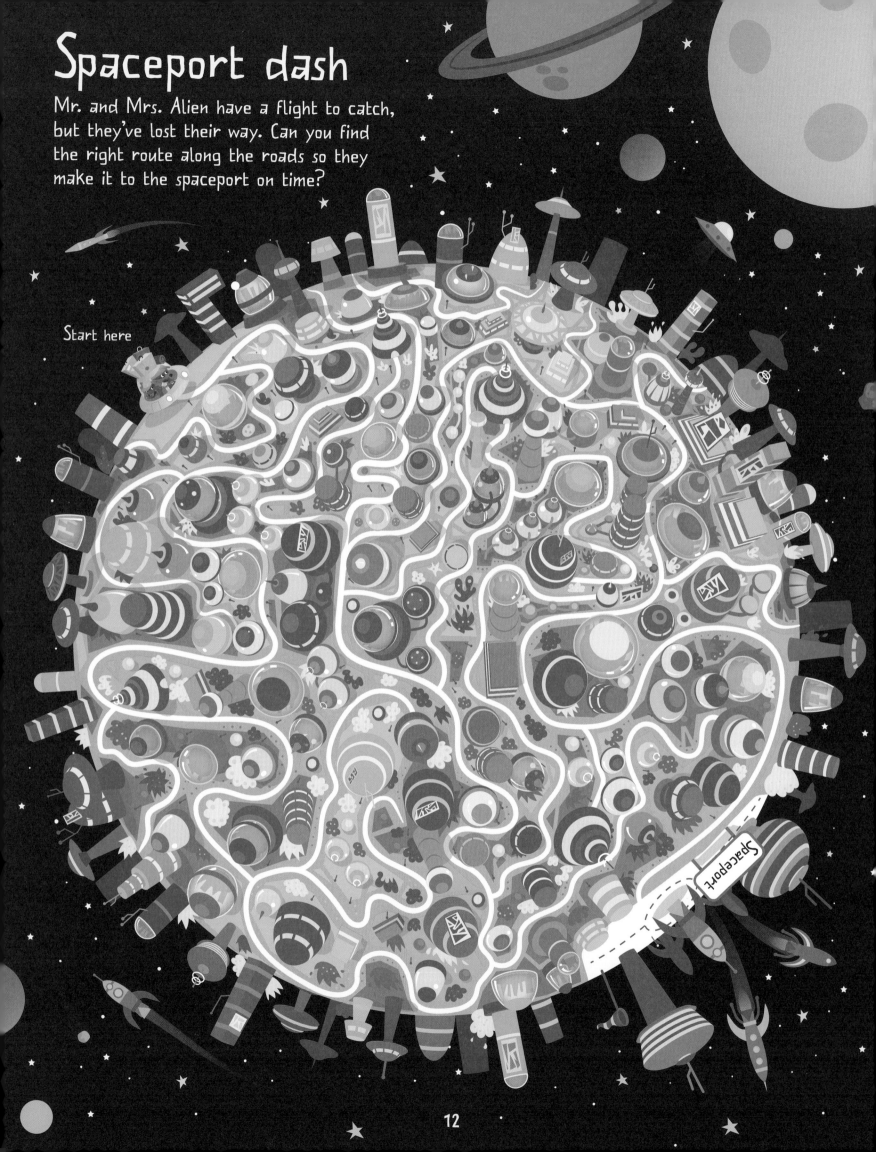

Rocket round trip

Take a tour of all three launch pads in order, finishing where you began. Avoid the blocked roads, and don't double back.

3

2

1

Start/Finish

Alarm alert

The air-safety alarm is faulty. Help the astronauts check its wiring by finding the circuit's path through the white cables and all the black detectors.

Detectors look like this.

AIR
SAFETY
ALARM
Start and
finish here

Galaxy game

Fly your saucer through all the gold and white stars to the ringed planet. Watch out for moons and meteors, and don't retrace your route.

Launch ladders

It's ten minutes to launch, and Frank must make his way along the ladders to reach the rocket's hatch – but they're not all linked. Which way should he go?

Frank

Probe pathway

A space probe has journeyed from Earth all the way to the outer edge of the Solar System. Which route did it take between the planets?

Space
probe

Hotel hurry

Seb's in a rush to join his friends in the pool, and doesn't want to be delayed by any of the other guests. Which way can he go to miss meeting anyone?

Pool

Observation deck

Seb

Radio rush

Guide the pink pod along the sky-cable network to the floating Radio Station in time for the alien's daily podcast. Avoid the meteors and traffic, though!

Pick-up problem

It's mayhem at the mall today. Can you help Felix find a path between the parked-up pods to collect his son, Simon?

Simon

Felix

22

Purpella pioneer

An astronaut is on an expedition to planet Purpella. Steer him along the interplanetary pathways so he can explore its surface.

Purpella

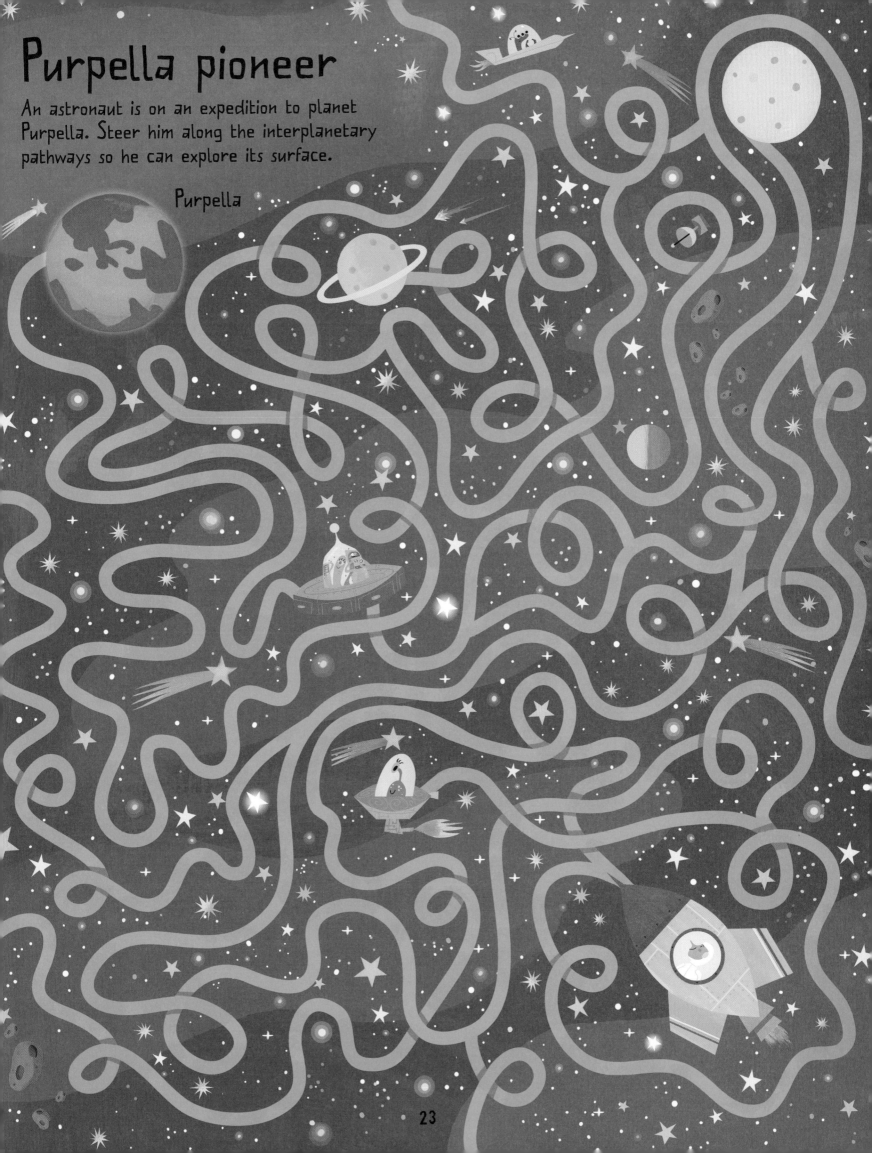

Stinky swamp

Help Zaphlack find his way back across the festering waters to his ship, avoiding the poisonous plants and the monsters lurking in the mire.

Zaphlack

Robot junkyard

Whoops! Scrapper has left his arm somewhere in the junkyard. Can you find it and pick out a path through the trash so he can collect it?

Scrapper

Alien approach

Scientists on Earth are trying to make contact with the alien spacecraft. Find the path their message must take along the wiggly radio waves to ask if the alien is friend or foe.

Galaxy shortcut

Two aliens are racing their rockets home. Vingo thinks the route between the starry clouds is shorter, avoiding rocks and planets. Zingo decides to fly along the galaxy's rainbow pathway. Who will reach home first?

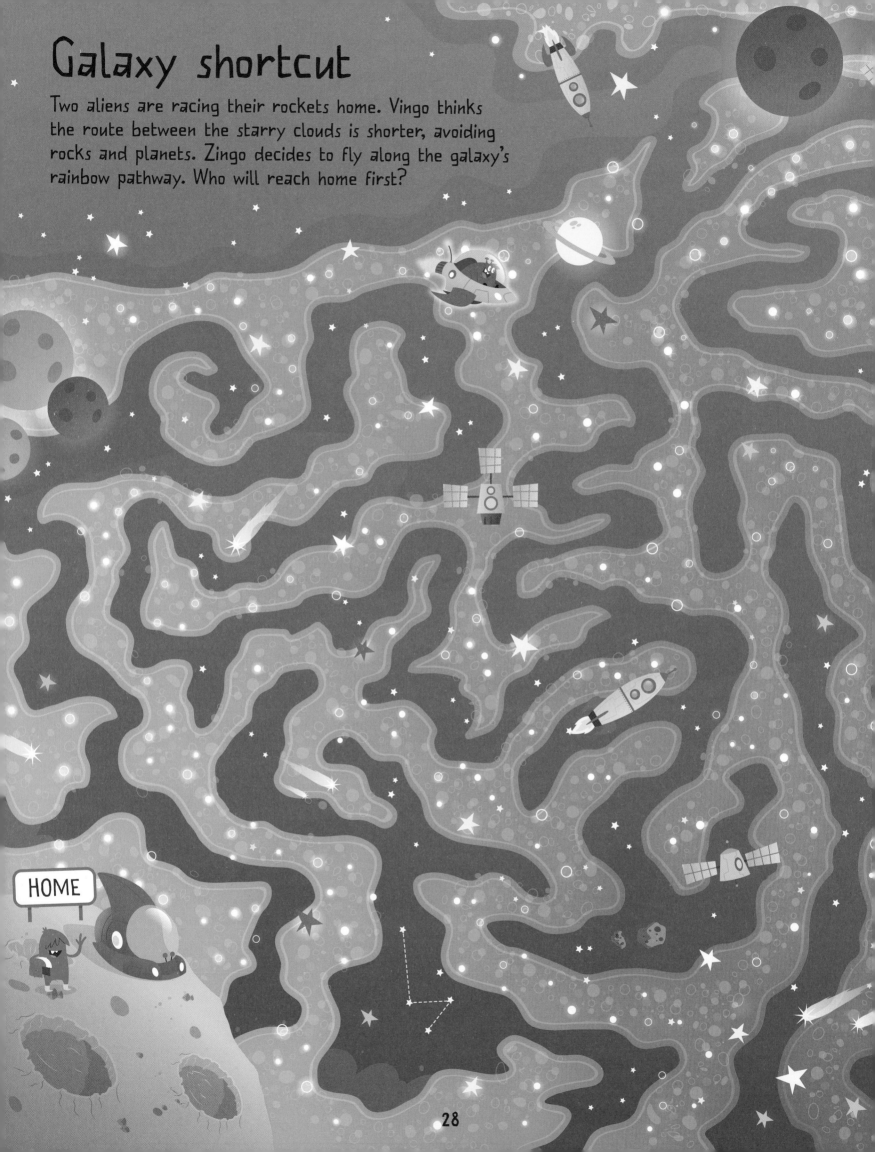

HOME

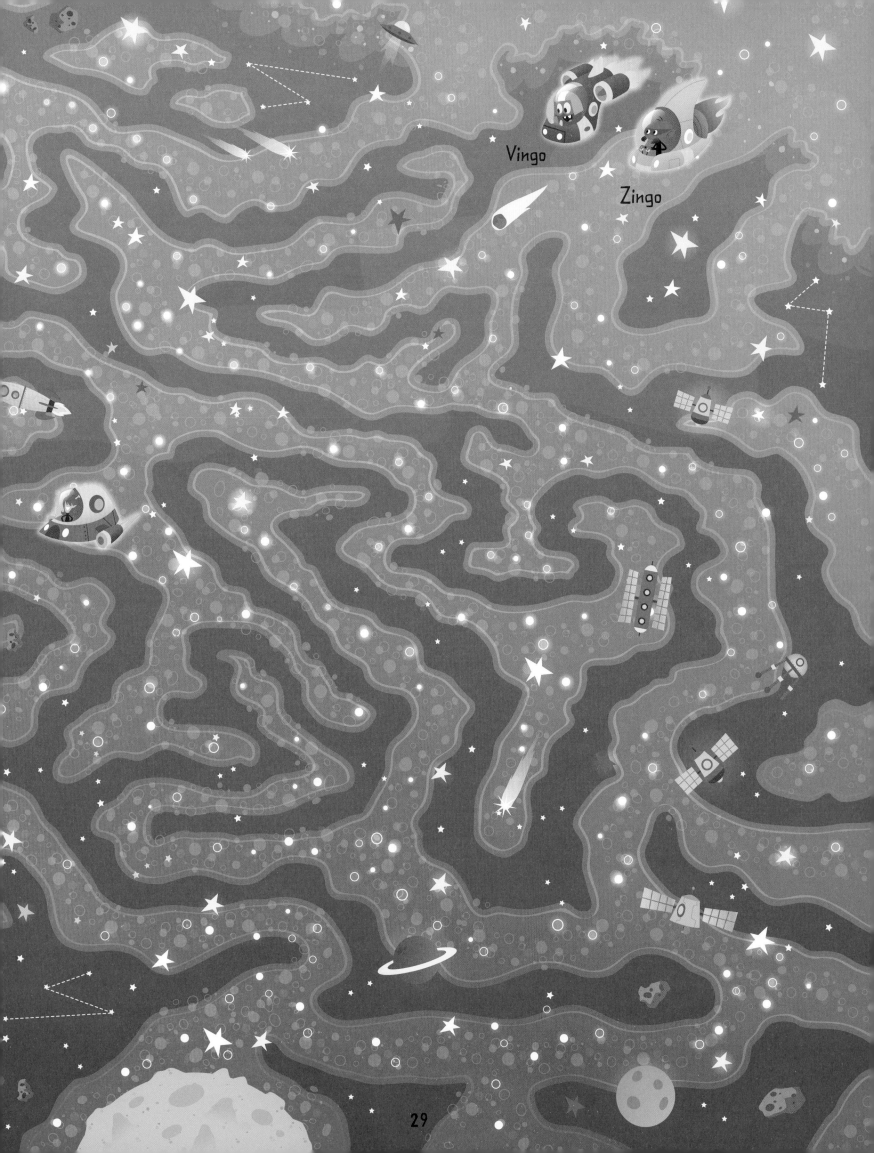

Vingo

Zingo

29

Bright beams

Guide the rocket safely down to land, avoiding the dangerously dazzling lights of the alien craft.

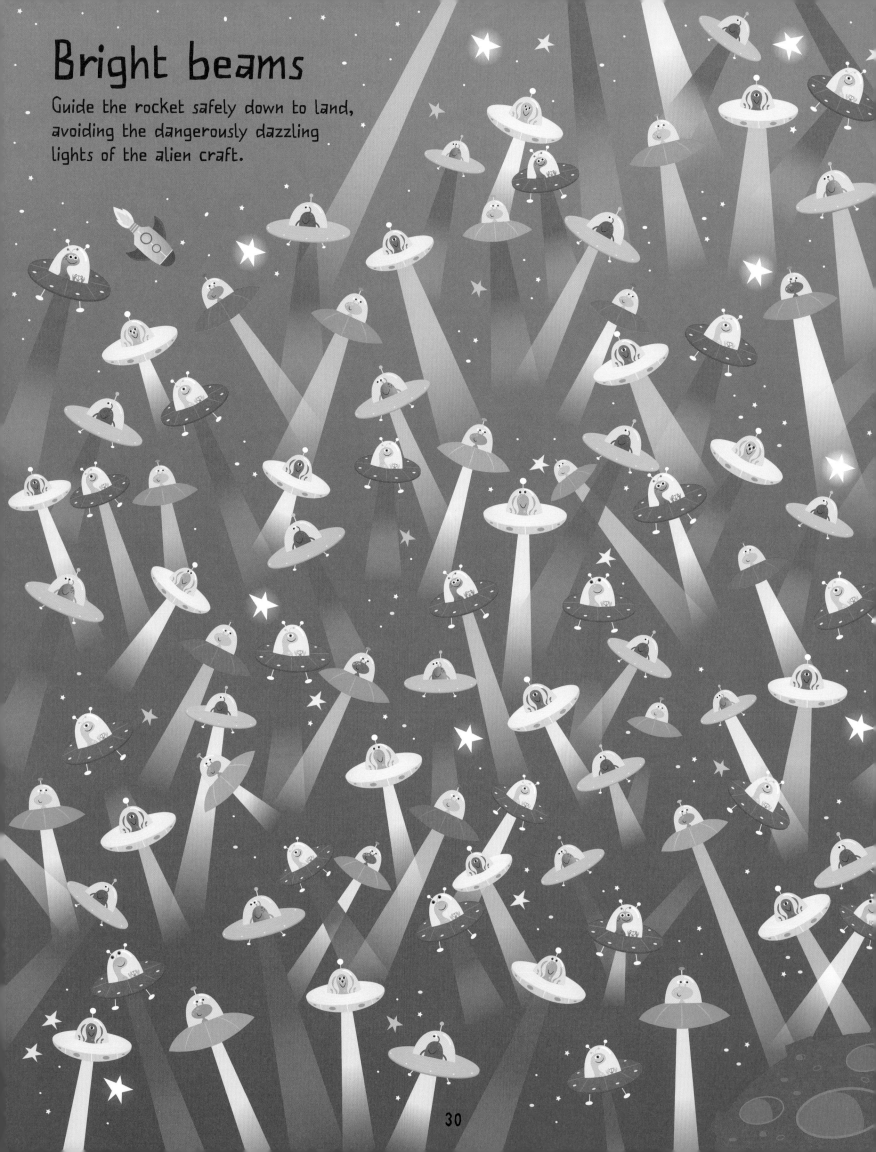

Crater collection

Jim has to collect samples from all the flagged craters on his way back to the spacecraft, but he must stick to the paths. Which route will take him to each crater just once?

Jim

Satellite repair

The astronaut is fixing this satellite's solar panel. Help her find a route over all the broken black cells she must mend – she can only move along the light-blue cells and can't double back.

Start

Finish

Dome roam

The man in the glass elevator wants to take his dog for a walk in the park. Which way must he go through the domes to get there?

Landing location

Help Mission Control guide the Space Shuttle along a safe flight path to one of the three landing zones. It can't fly through the areas of bad weather, marked by the orange dots.

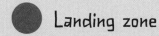 Landing zone

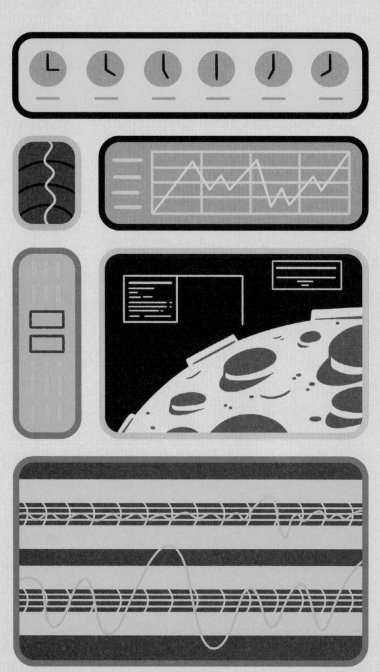

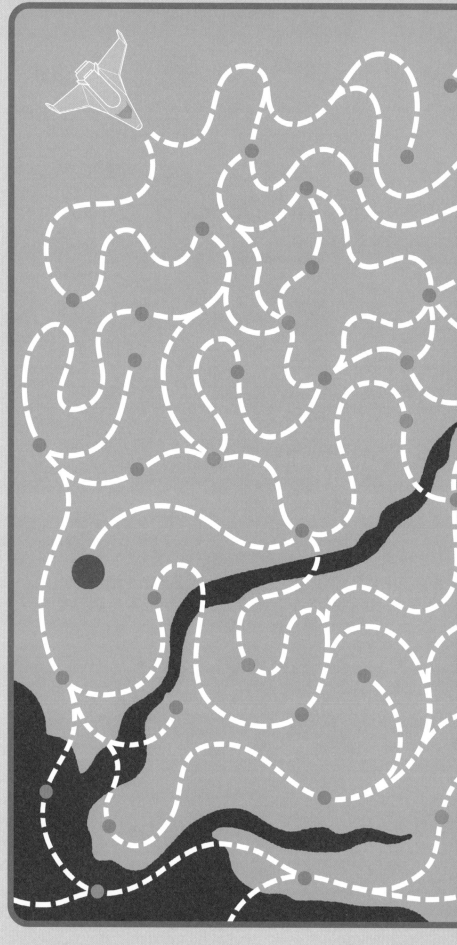

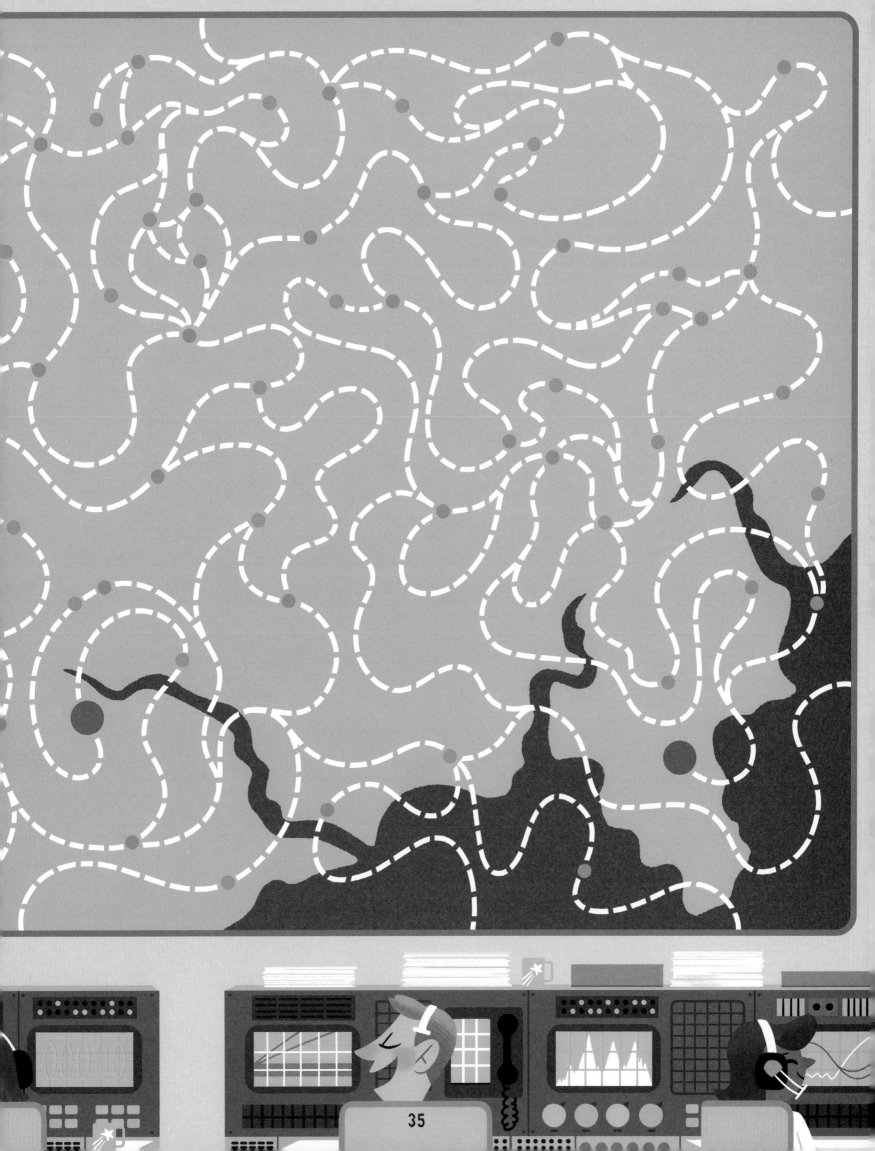

World of Space

Maisie's ticket to this space museum allows her to visit each room just once. Plan a route so she can see all of the exhibits, finishing at the Space Shuttle.

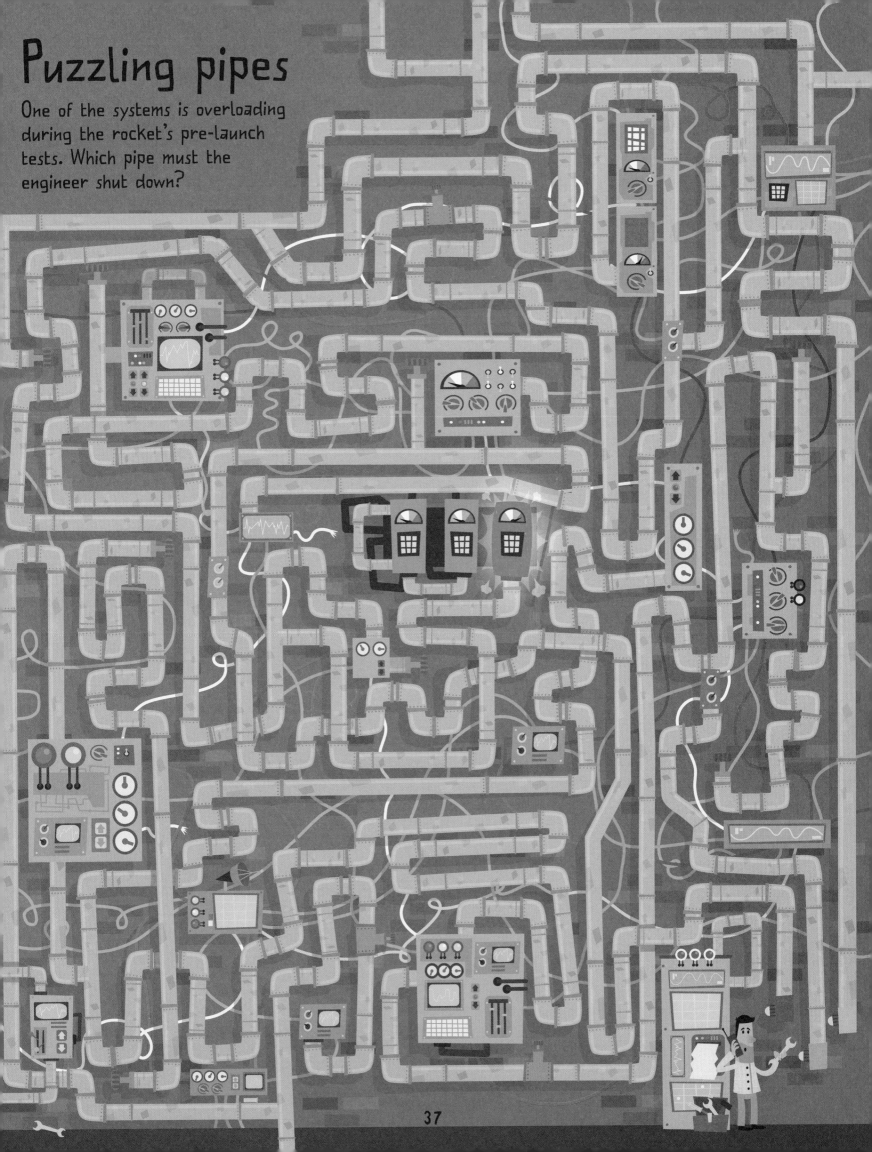

Puzzling pipes

One of the systems is overloading during the rocket's pre-launch tests. Which pipe must the engineer shut down?

Constellation quest

Help the space adventurer return to his home planet after his long voyage, flying from star to star through the constellations. He must avoid the dying red ones, however, or he may lose his way.

Start here

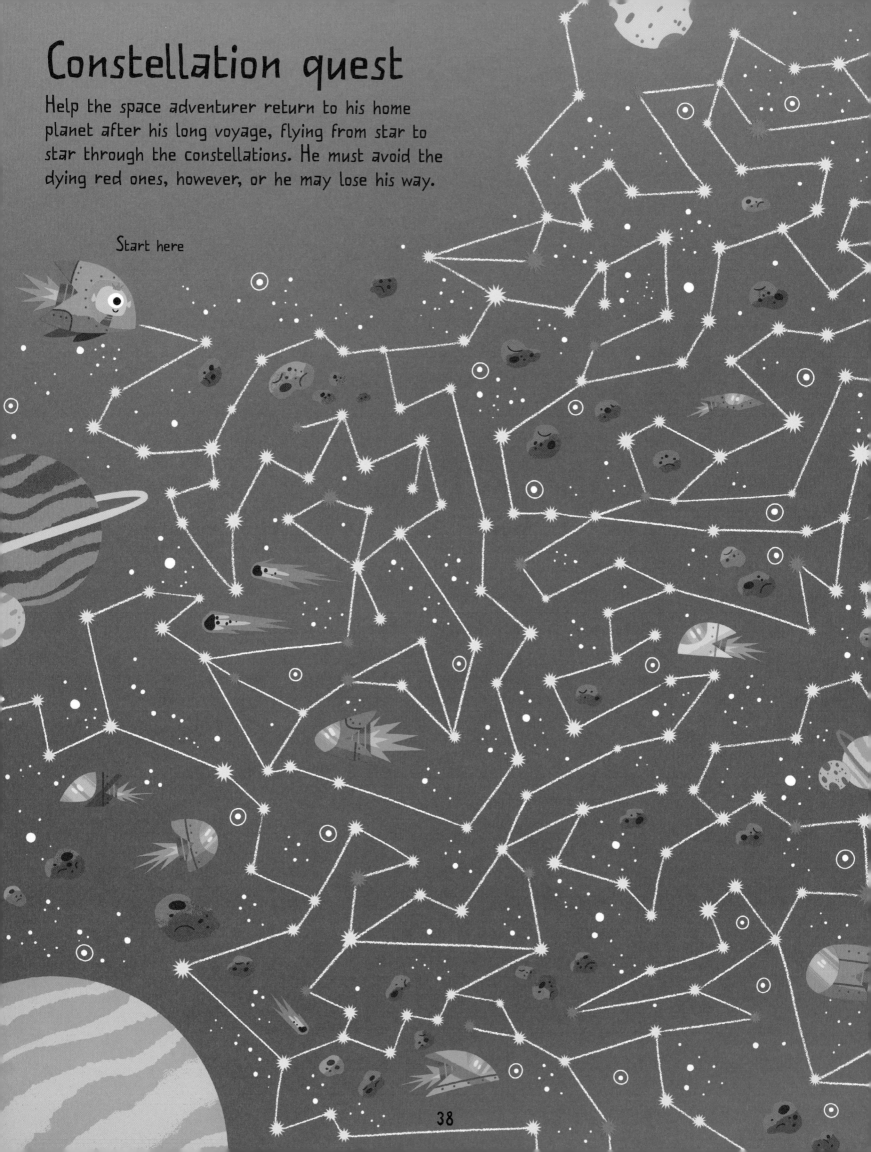

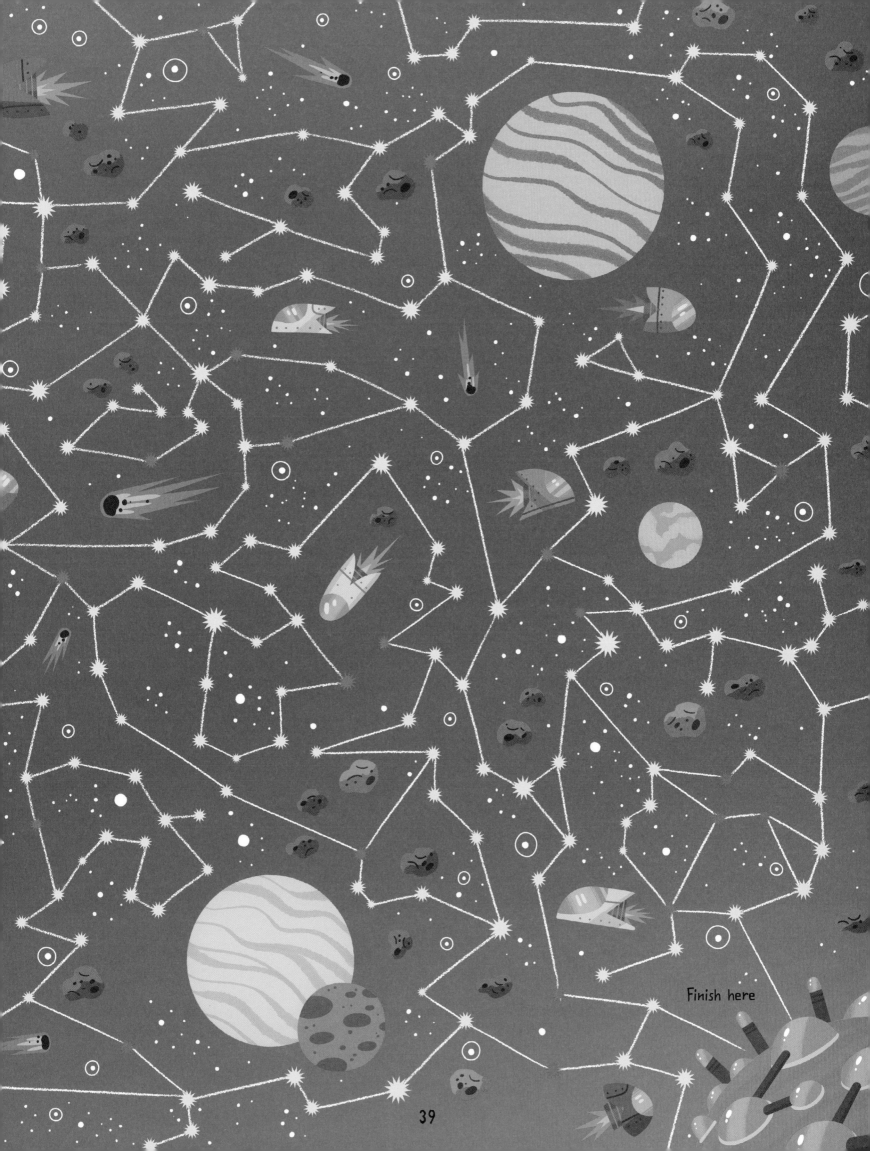

Finish here

39

Life on Mars

Guide the Mars Rover back along its tracks to Laboratory One, collecting data from all five astronauts on the way. Its path can cross over itself but it can't take the same trail twice.

Mars Rover

Flying saucers

Help Zurg fly between the stars to the pink planet, passing all his friends on the way, and without retracing any part of his route.

Zurg

Sizzling circuits

Hurry! The ship's circuits are overheating. Can you find a path to the backup system in time, avoiding the sparking connections and white-hot wires?

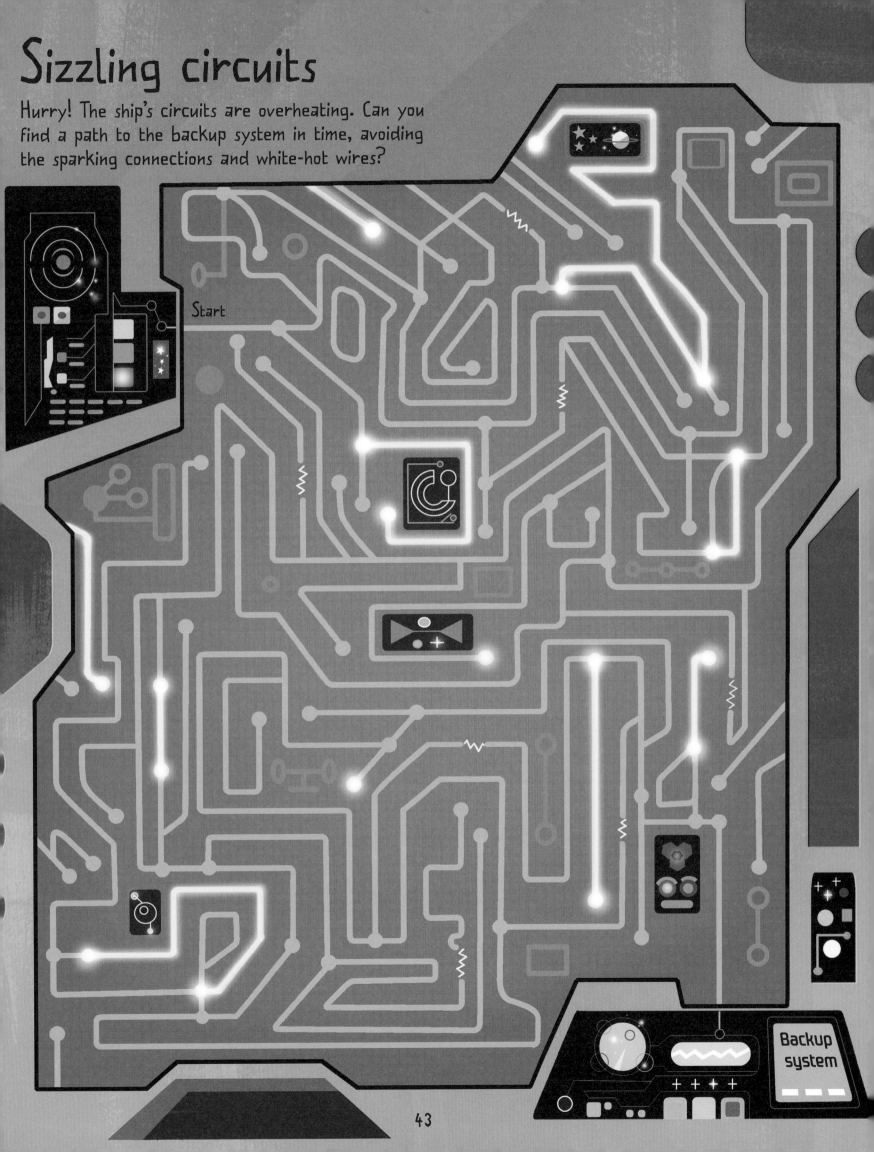

Start

Backup system

Tricky teleporters

Help Ed use the teleport pads to reach the ship's control room. Each pad can take him to any other pad with a matching sign. (His gravity suit lets him float across gaps or along clear paths between the decks.)

Teleport pads look like this.

Ed

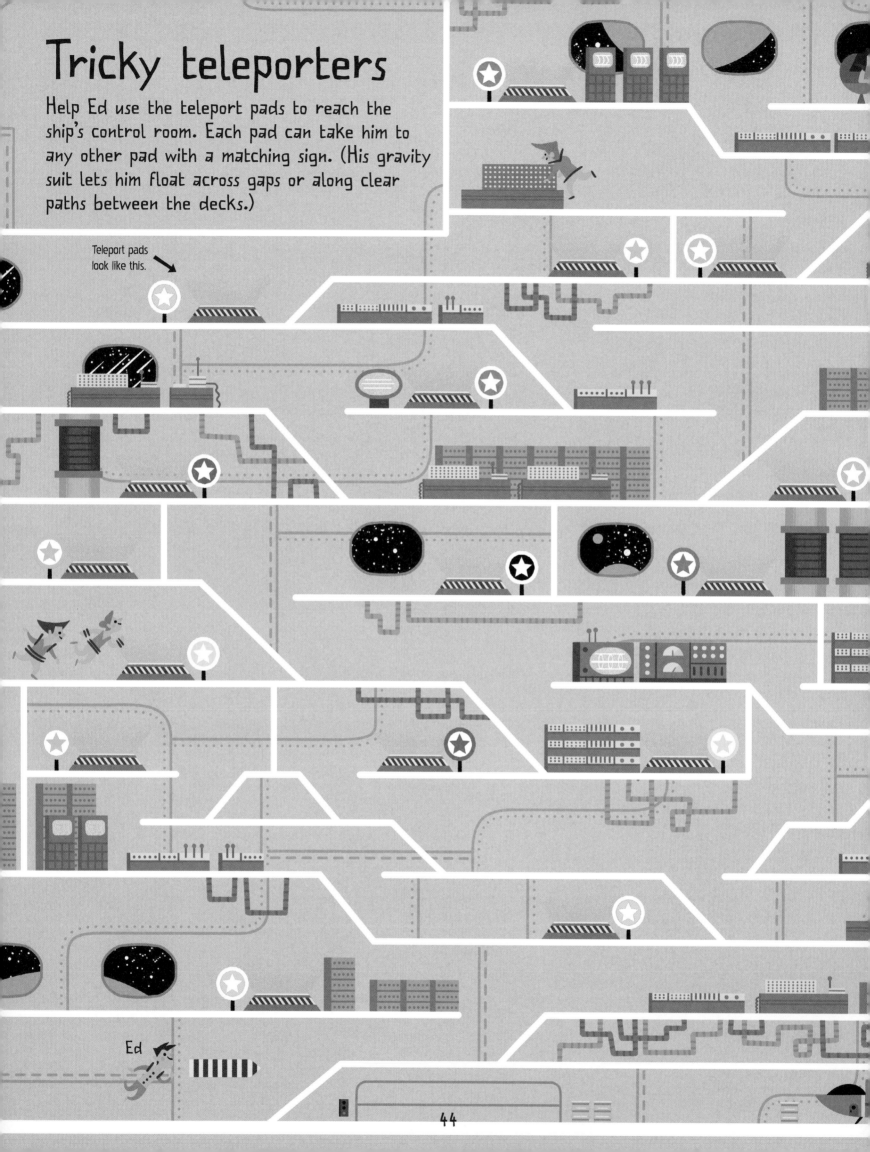

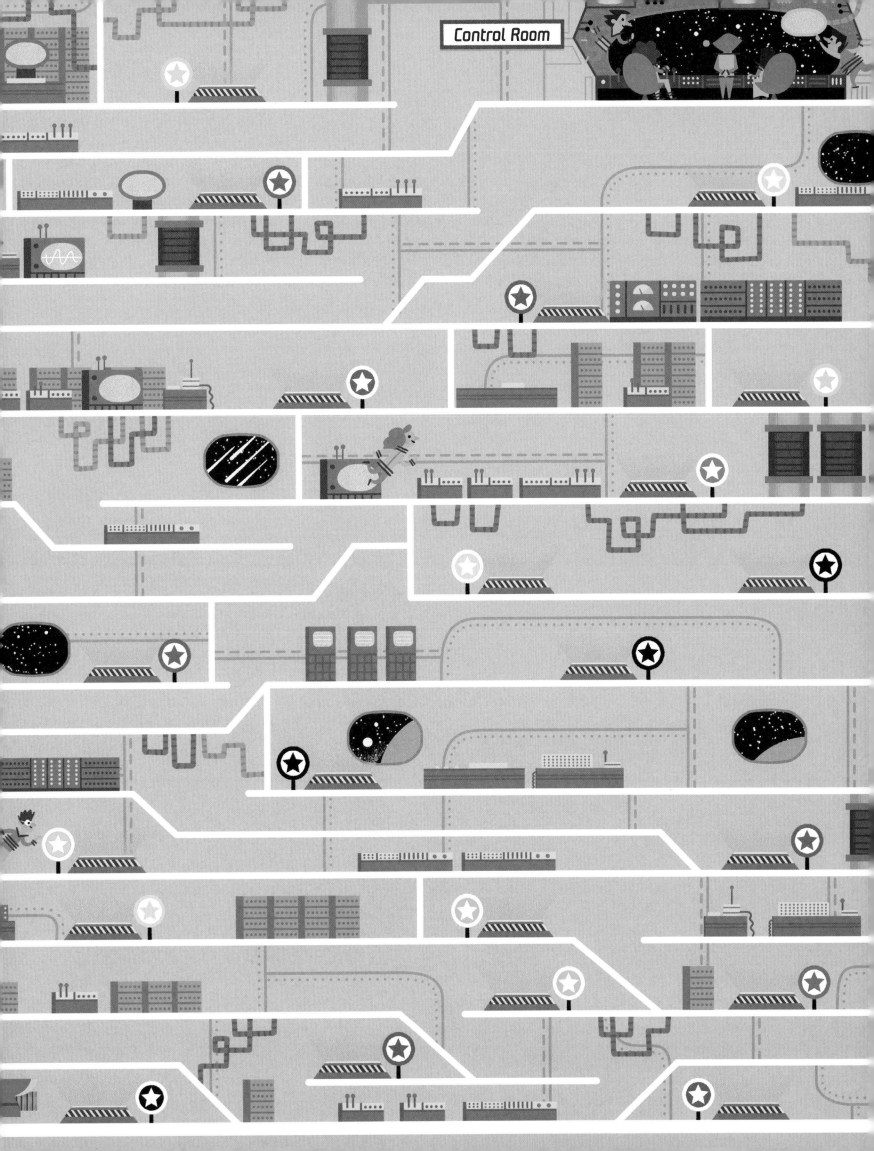

Control Room

Rocky rings

Guide Glissa along a clear route between the planet's rings of rock to join Selenia on its surface.

Glissa

Selenia

Robot network

These space robots help each other recharge by linking up in a long line. Find the path the electricity will take from Sparks, who's fully charged, to Greta.

Sparks

Greta

Ravine recharge

Bogon's buggy battery is running low, but he can only use the green recharging points. Can you find a route that will take him to one?

Bogon

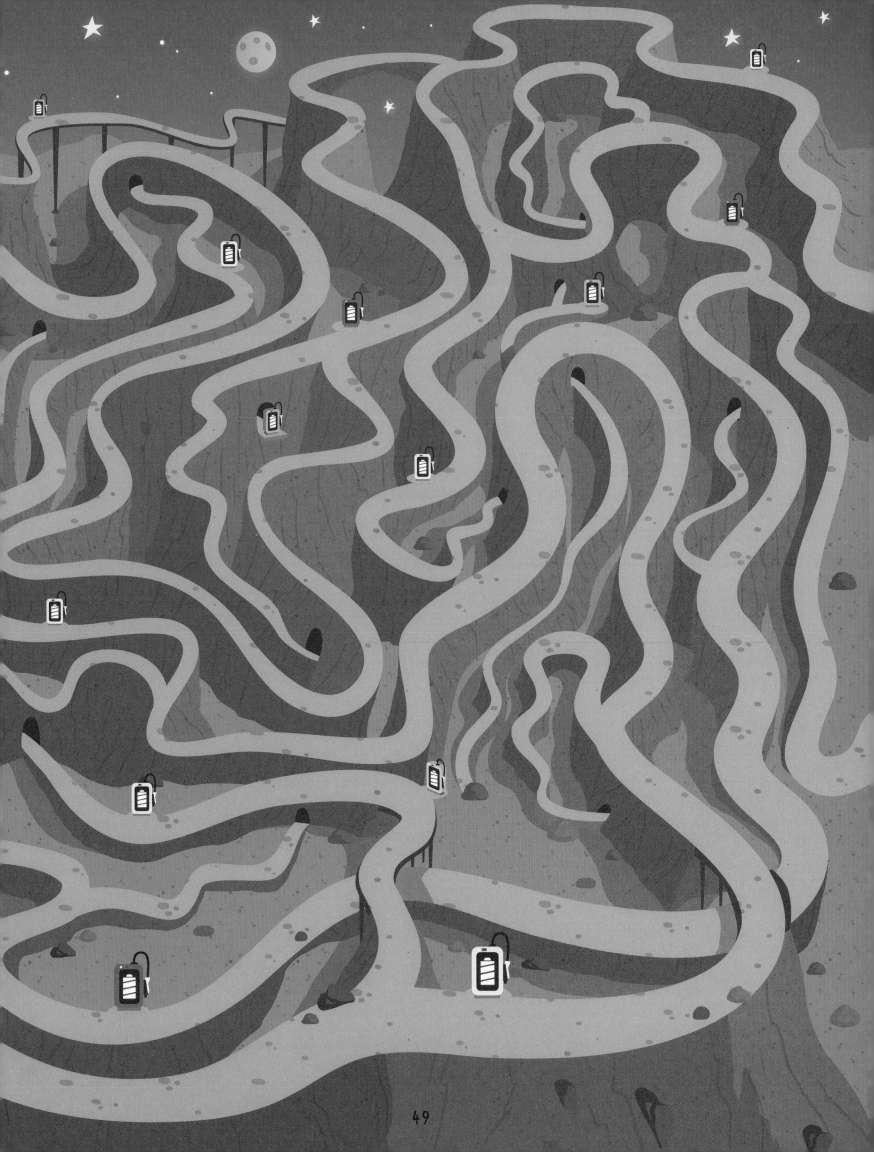

Challenging chart

Plot a flight path to the Red Planet carefully. You can only fly through completely empty grid squares, and you can't move diagonally between them.

Destination

Start

Black hole escape

Help the approaching rocket safely navigate the
black hole's powerful pull without being sucked
into the middle. Be careful not to crash into
other vessels in the vortex!

Intergalactica Space Park

Park your pod, buy a balloon, then wander around all the star attractions, bagging a souvenir on your way out. You can pass other visitors, but don't revisit any path or ride, and avoid the Cosmic Coaster right after your lunch!

Astra Slide

Human House

Space Burger Bar

Cosmic Coaster

Rocket
Revolution

Souvenirs

Observation
Tower

Exit

Entrance

Solar satellites

Follow the flight paths to find out which one the Sunseeker satellite must travel along to join the others in orbit around this faraway sun.

Sunseeker

Dangerous debris

Without warning, the little rocket has been engulfed in a deadly galactic storm. Can you steer it between the fiery flashes and trails back to the mothership?

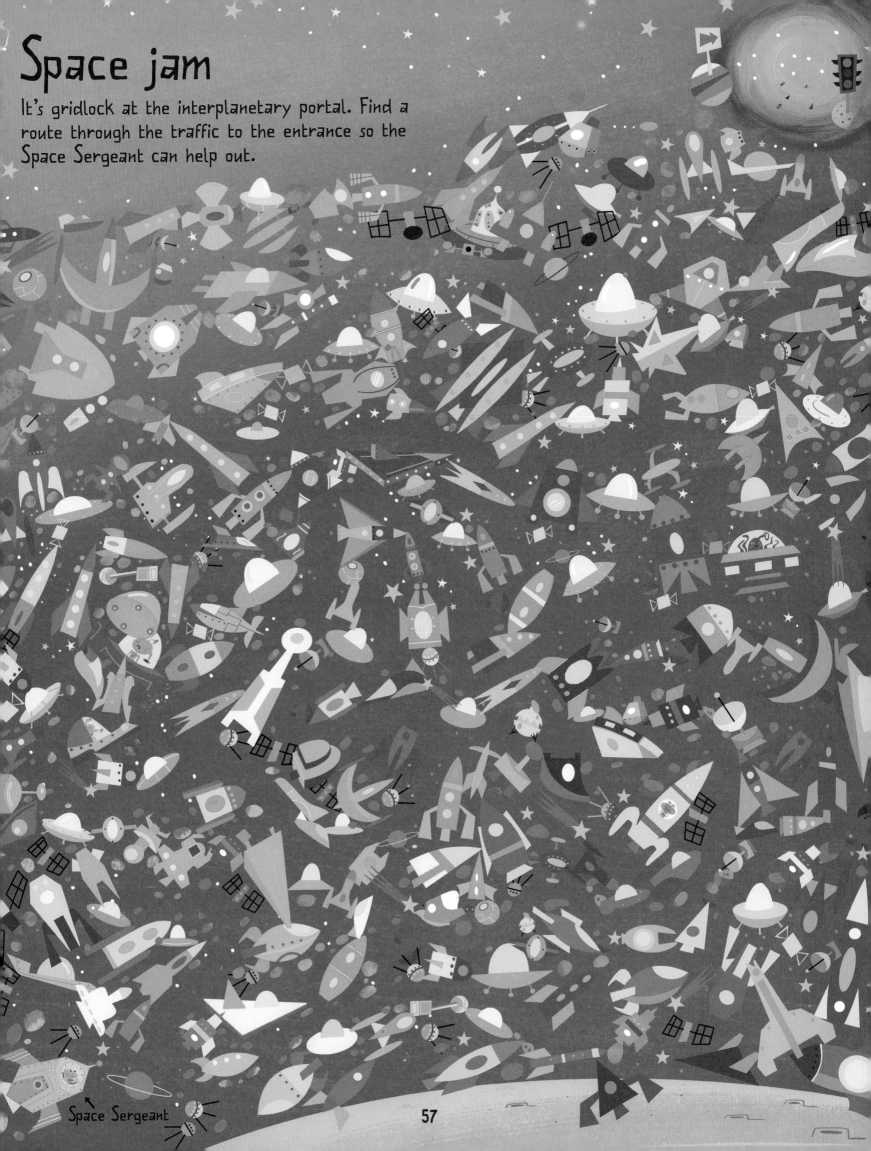

Space jam

It's gridlock at the interplanetary portal. Find a route through the traffic to the entrance so the Space Sergeant can help out.

Space Sergeant

Planetary tour

Map a route from Nerilla to Lunos, visiting all 31 planets between them, and stopping for lunch on Planet Burger at exactly halfway. Stick to the starry trails, and don't revisit any path or planet.

Nerilla

Lunos

Alien interface

The red alien has a message for his orange friend, but only the smiling aliens will pass it on, and they can't communicate diagonally. Find a path for the message to travel along.

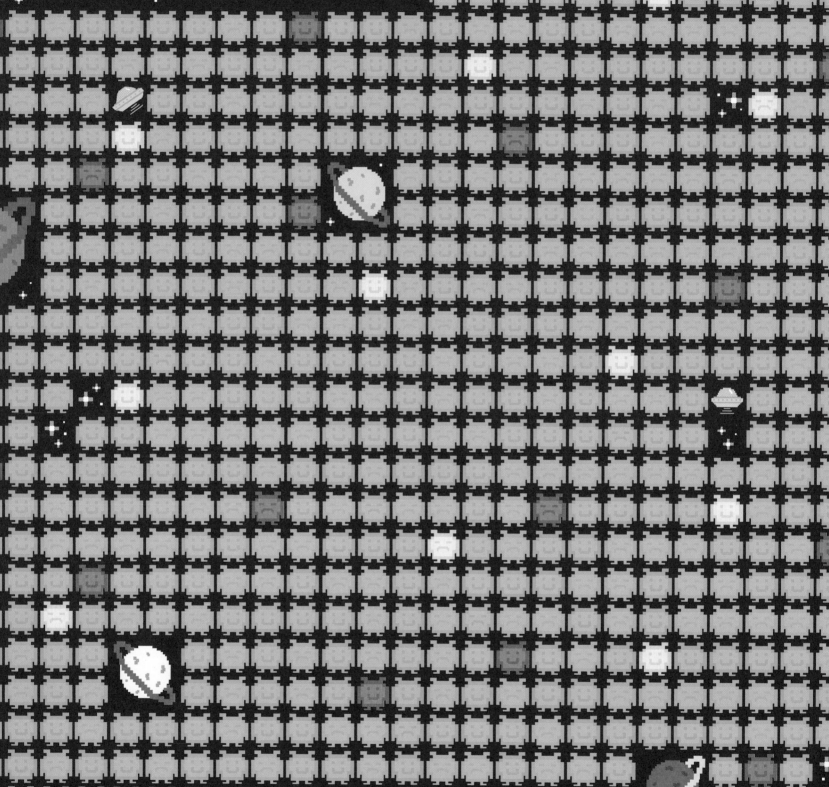

2. Alien evasion
3. Into the blast zone

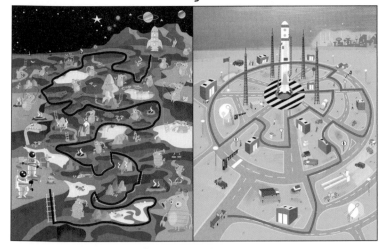

4. Metropolis skyline
5. Spacewalk tangle

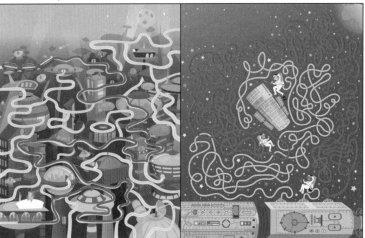

6-7. Cosmic racers

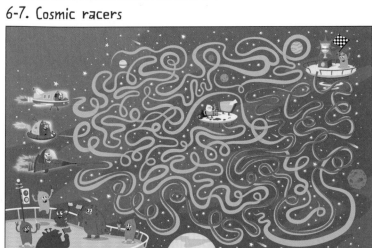

8. Fly the flag
9. Dish dilemma

10-11. Chasm quandary

12. Spaceport dash
13. Rocket round trip

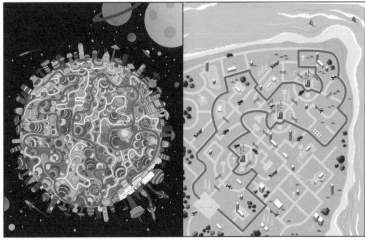

14-15. Alarm alert

16. Galaxy game
17. Launch ladders

18-19. Probe pathway

20. Hotel hurry   21. Radio rush

22. Pick-up problem   23. Purpella pioneer

24-25. Stinky swamp

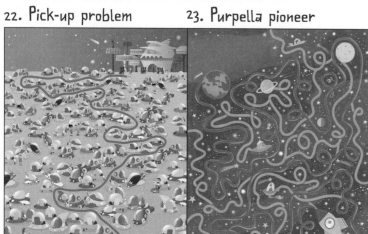

26. Robot junkyard   27. Alien approach

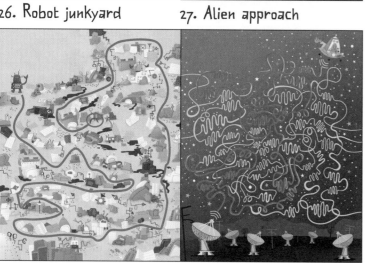

28-29. Galaxy shortcut

Zingo will win

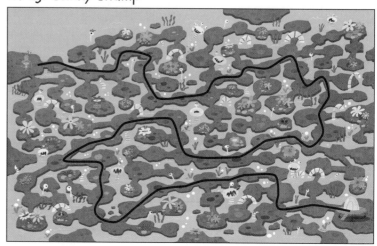

30. Bright beams   31. Crater collection

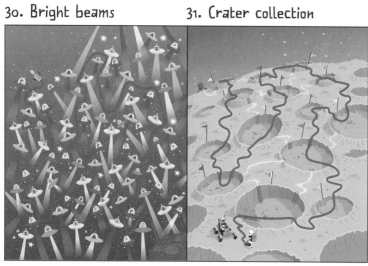

32. Satellite repair   33. Dome roam

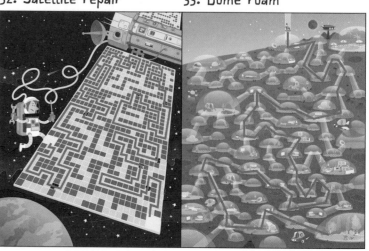

34-35. Landing location

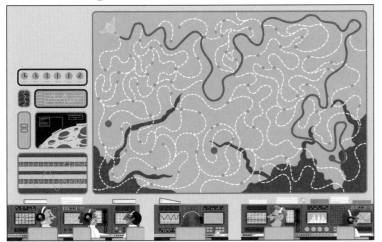

36. World of Space 37. Puzzling pipes

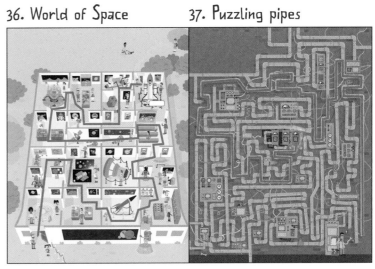

38-39. Constellation quest

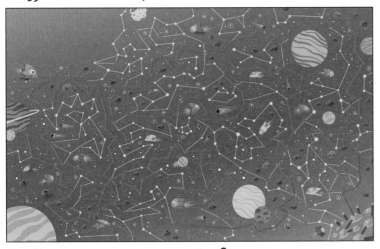

40-41. Life on Mars

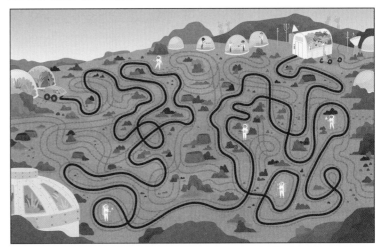

42. Flying saucers 43. Sizzling circuits

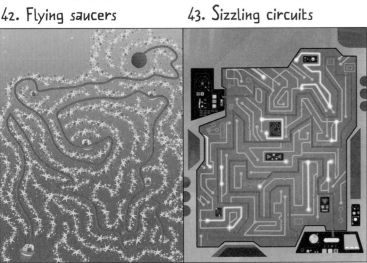

44-45. Tricky teleporters

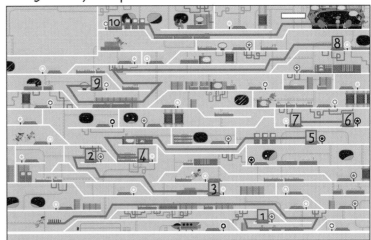

46. Rocky rings 47. Robot network

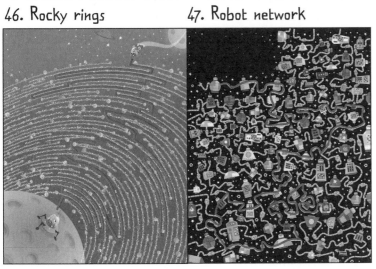

48-49. Ravine recharge

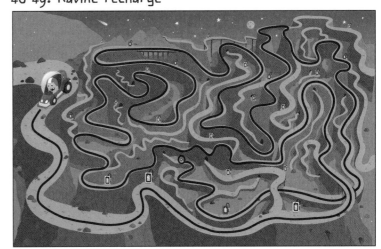

50. Challenging chart

51. Black hole escape

52-53. Intergalactica Space Park

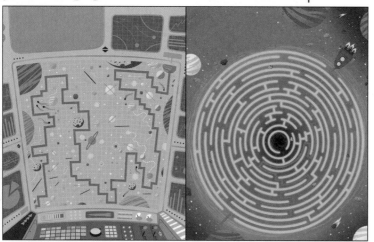

54-55. Solar satellites

56. Dangerous debris

57. Space jam

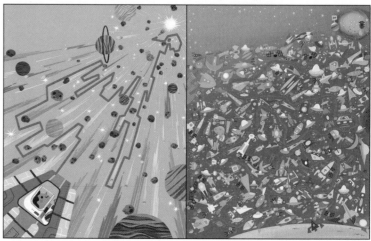

58-59. Planetary tour

60. Alien interface

Acknowledgements

Additional designs by Laura Hammonds and Sharon Cooper

Cover design by Kate Rimmer

Edited by Kirsteen Robson and Sam Taplin

First published in 2016 by Usborne Publishing Ltd. 83–85 Saffron Hill, London ECIN 8RT, England.
First published in America in 2016. UE. Printed in China.